I AM
MAGIC

How To Create Your Best Life

Maria Robins

I AM MAGIC
How To Create Your Best Life

Requests for publication should be addressed to:

Altreya Publishing Ltd
PO Box 90 256, Victoria Street West
Auckland, New Zealand 1142

ISBN-13: 978-0-473-38192-9

DEDICATION

This book is dedicated to us all.

With love.

I'll see it when I believe it

Dr Wayne W. Dyer

Magic is believing in yourself. If you can do that, you can make anything real

Goethe

I don't know what it was about May the 10th
But suddenly I awoke around 3.00 am
A thought tumbled in just as clear as a bell
On how to help people to do really well
Urging me to write the words down
So from bed I rose and a pen I found
Here's the story that was told to me
At the time of thirteen minutes past three

Believe

It's all to do with what we think

It really is the one true link

Between a happy life and one that's sad

We can think it good, or we can think it bad

What we believe is what we get

It's mind over matter, lest you forget

What do you mean by that, you say?

Well let me put it to you this way...

Our thoughts are like a dripping tap

A few drops are OK and not much of that

But more than a few fill the sink to the top

And the next thing you know
you find you can't stop

Thinking about all the things that are wrong

Instead of the great things you've
got going on

The sink overflows and turns into a pool

So think only good things, that is the rule

Or let me put it another way

In case you're not sure what
I'm trying to say

Each thought that you have is a jigsaw piece

That joins with the next, like a flock of geese

One on its own cannot do too much

But put them together and there's
power as such

Like the geese joining forces
as they fly along

One with the next, is what makes
them strong

How many times do you think I AM...?

Something or other... consider if you can

How many times do you say to yourself

I AM happy, I AM sad, or...

I'm something else?

I AM rich, I AM poor, I AM feeling great

I AM getting a cold, I'm putting on weight

And what happens when you think
all these things?

Well just like magic, that's what life brings

Using the words I AM is a power

One drop in a bucket hour by hour

If you've thought I AM happy

Then that's what you'll feel

If you've thought I AM angry

Then that's what you'll make real

Which one would you rather be?

It's easy to do and your thoughts are free!

The power of positive thinking you say

You've got it! So now let me put it this way...

When you think or say the words I AM

You are tapping into a Master Plan

Like having your very own magic show

Abracadabra-can, here we go

You don't have to know how it will be

Just believe it and feel it, then wait and see

Like planting a seed, your thought might
take some time

But be sure if you say I AM first,
it will thrive

Say the words I AM loved, oh yes I AM

Then imagine the very same thing,
if you can

You cannot fail in this you see

Because what you think, is what will be

So only think good and never think bad

Make yourself happy, rather than sad

Say, 'the Master Magician in my life I AM'

I create only good things, oh yes I CAN

And if I'm experiencing
tough things right now

I focus on good and know that somehow

Great things will happen, as long as I trust

The Universe gives what I believe,
yes it must!

Not only for me but also for others

Mothers and fathers, sisters and brothers

Friends and family, plants and pets

What I AM focusing on, is what I will get

And here's where you must pay
real attention

Because this one is very important
to mention

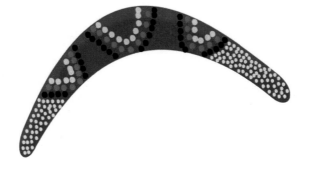

When you think of your friends
and fellow men

You must only think of the good I AM

If you think ill of others you will get the boot

This is a point that is really quite moot

As sure as if you had kicked yourself

It will boomerang back and make itself felt

Think of this and you'll know what I mean

When I remind you of the pinball machine

You pull a lever and the ball flies out

And pings around here,
and there, and about

But no matter how many places it darts

It always returns itself back to the start

Your thoughts are exactly the same as that
pinball

They go out and return to the source of it all

And since you're the one who is
pulling the lever

Don't you think you had better
become a believer?

That good vibes will ping out, around,
and come back

But so too will bad vibes, exactly like that

You must only think of things that are kind

For yourself and for others,
for all of mankind

Because that energy then goes out
to the world

And circles right back around to us all

Remember, thoughts are like seeds so be
careful to sow

Only good ones and then have faith
they will grow

And if you don't see the results straightaway

Be sure that they're destined to
show up one day

Pluck out the negative,
unkind thought weeds

And make sure to replace them with
happy thought seeds

NON-SPECIFIC things are best

The Great I AM will take care of the rest

I am happy!

Here's some examples of what you can say:

I AM loved, I AM happy

I AM feeling good today

Replace I AM worried, with I AM so calm

That way your words can do you no harm

Instead of saying I'm no good at this

Say, I AM achieving all that I wish

I AM seeing this thing happen with ease

It's all falling right into place if you please!

WISDOM

POWER

VISION

FEELING

So let's check once more before I go
That you have all the tools you need
to know...
What you focus on, you expand
It really is part of Life's Divine Plan

The way to bring your dreams to fruition

Is all contained here in this easy tuition

First of all **think** it

Secondly **see** it

And thirdly make sure to let yourself **feel** it

If you say I AM happy, then think of a time

Where you felt extra happy,
to bring that in line

With the happiness you want
to experience today

Then *feel* that same energy to
bring it your way

Once more...

Think it, and ***see*** it

Then let yourself ***feel*** it

I AM grateful for
the sun on my face

I AM grateful for
the wind cooling
me down

I AM grateful for
the rain watering
the grass

And if you should want to hurry things up

Try filling up your gratitude cup

Make sure you're not proud,
boastful, or vain

Just be grateful for all that is good,
that's your aim

Find ten things that you can be
glad of each day

And when you do this, more will then
come your way

The more you can think of only good things

The more you will find that
that's what life brings

Now you've got it, I AM most pleased to see

That what you believe, is what will be

Just one word of caution before I depart

An important last piece of advice
from the heart

Don't think you are better than anyone ever

This is a no-no - in fact it's a never

No matter our skin tone, our race,
or our name

Inside we are all just exactly the same

And the people in life
who most irk or upset you

Are the very same ones
you must send the most love to

Wish them the same happy things as for you

And you might find they gradually change,
yes it's true

Remember it all goes out, around, and
comes back

So you will be the recipient of that

The more you can think of
and do better things

The more to yourself and the world
you will bring

Be as kind to each other
as you want to receive

And that's what you'll get, you just have to

BELIEVE.

To receive updates on new I AM releases please email:
altreyapublishing@gmail.com

If you found this book helpful, please consider leaving a review to help spread the word – thank you!

www.iamjournals.com

www.facebook.com/iamjournals

About the Author

Maria Robins was born in the Scottish heritage town of Dunedin, New Zealand and currently lives in Auckland, NZ. She loves words and writing and books, along with long walks at sunset and all things nature.

Her goal is to inspire as many people as possible to believe in the power of maintaining a positive mindset and grateful attitude so that they can enjoy their most joyful and meaningful lives.

Other books by Maria Robins

Is your child anxious or do you find yourself stressed and overwhelmed at times?

It's all too easy to get bogged down in worry, anxiety and fear these days. Sometimes we simply need a little reminder of a few simple things we can do to help us stay calm during stressful stuff. I AM Calm is written in a whimsical rhyming style with corresponding illustrations, and contains easy coping strategies that use the combination of a positive mindset and basic breathing techniques, to help kids conquer their worries and fears.

Suitable for all ages, including those grown ups who might just need a gentle, calming reminder of their own!

Other books by Maria Robins

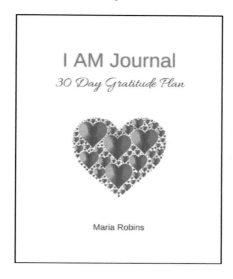

Finding appreciation is one of the nicest things you can do for yourself and for those around you.

Not only is it good to focus on the things in life that you are grateful for but it has the added bonus of attracting more good things into your life.

The I AM Journal 30 Day Gratitude Plan is designed to help you focus on the positive aspects in your life by writing them down each day and reviewing them on a weekly basis.

At the end of the 30 days you will be amazed how many things you can find to be grateful for.

Notes:

Notes:

Made in the USA
Las Vegas, NV
05 March 2021

19084172R00038